FAR-OUT and UNUSUAL

Miniature Horses

pets

Cool Pets!

Enslow Elementary

an imprint of

Enslow Publishers, Inc.
40 Industrial Road
Box 398
Berkeley Heights, NJ 07922
USA

http://www.enslow.com

Alvin and Virginia Silverstein
and Laura Silverstein Nunn

Enslow Elementary, an imprint of Enslow Publishers, Inc.

Enslow Elementary® is a registered trademark of Enslow Publishers, Inc.

Library of Congress Cataloging-in-Publication Data
Silverstein, Alvin.
  Miniature horses : cool pets! / Alvin Silverstein, Virginia Silverstein and Laura Silverstein Nunn.
      p. cm. — (Far-out and unusual pets)
  Includes index.
  Summary: "Provides basic information about miniature horses and keeping them as pets"
—Provided by publisher.
  ISBN 978-0-7660-3880-6
  1. Miniature horses—Juvenile literature. I. Silverstein, Virginia B. II. Nunn, Laura Silverstein. III.
Title.
  SF293.M56S53 2012
  636.1—dc22

                                        2011006058

Future editions:

Paperback ISBN 978-1-4644-0125-1

ePUB ISBN 978-1-4645-1032-8

PDF ISBN 978-1-4646-1032-5

Printed in China

012012 Leo Paper Group, Heshan City, Guangdong, China

10 9 8 7 6 5 4 3 2 1

To Our Readers: We have done our best to make sure all Internet Addresses in this book were
active and appropriate when we went to press. However, the author and the publisher have no
control over and assume no liability for the material available on those Internet sites or on other Web
sites they may link to. Any comments or suggestions can be sent by e-mail to comments@enslow.com
or to the address on the back cover.

Illustration Credits: © 2011 by Gerald Kelley (www.geraldkelley.com)

Photo Credits: Alamy: © Cultura, p. 35, © Juniors Bildarchiv, p. 14, © Mark J. Barrett, p. 21;
P Images: Jim Beckel, p. 38, Jim Cole, pp. 8, 12, Julie Lewis, p. 6, Kevin Kinzley, p. 41, Scott
Heckel, p. 44; iStockphoto.com: © Alina Solovyova-Vincent, p. 19, © Debra Feinman, p. 27,
© Michelle Harvey, p. 15 (mini); Mandi Wright/MCT/Landov, p.43; Mary F. Calvert/The
Washington Times/Landov, p. 39; Newspix/Rex/Rex USA, Courtesy Everett Collection, p. 24; Pete
Markham, p. 10; Roland Weihrauch/dpa/Landov, p. 17 (top); Shutterstock.com, pp. 1, 4, 15 (pony),
17 (bottom), 25, 29, 30, 40.

Cover Photo: Shutterstock.com

Contents

A miniature horse
is a great choice
for a pet.

1

Pint-Size Horses

Have you ever begged your parents for a horse? Who could resist such a beautiful animal? But owning a horse is *a lot* of work. Horses are really big animals. You can't cuddle up to one at night. It needs to be outside with lots of room to run around. Keeping a horse also costs a lot of money.

If only these big beauties came in smaller sizes. Wouldn't it be cool to have one about the size of a dog? Luckily, pint-size horses really do exist. They are not ponies. They are a different kind of horse, called miniature horses. Many people call them mini horses, or minis for short.

Miniature horses love company.

Mini horses are popular pets. They look like regular horses, but they are *much* smaller. They are very sweet and gentle. They will even follow you around like a puppy dog!

Owning a mini horse is not like owning a dog, though. Sure, it's small enough to bring inside your house. But a mini horse is still a horse. It needs to be outside. It needs a lot less room and food compared to a regular-size horse, though. A mini horse would be happy in a person's backyard, with a shed for shelter. It will also eat much less than larger horses eat.

Still, keeping mini horses is a big responsibility. They take a lot more time and money to care for than a cat or dog. But many mini horse owners would say that it's worth it.

What would it be like to own a mini horse? Read on and find out what makes miniature horses such far-out and unusual pets.

Far Out!

An adult mini horse weighs an average of 150 pounds (60 kg). That's less than what a Saint Bernard weighs. The Saint Bernard is one of the largest dog breeds. Males can weigh up to 200 pounds (91 kg) or more!

2

A New Pet Craze?

Why are miniature horses so small? Did they not grow right? Are they sick? Mini horses are not small because there is something wrong with them. They are supposed to be that way. They are just as healthy as regular-size horses. Mini horses are simply a different breed of horse.

You might think that keeping mini horses is a new pet craze. But miniature horses have actually been around for a very long time. In fact, people have been keeping these little horses for hundreds of years!

The First Mini Horse Pets

The first miniature horse pets go back as early as the 1600s. These little horses were specially bred as pets for the kings and queens of Europe. The horses' small size made them easy to handle. They made great companions for the young princes and princesses. Mini horses were also used in England and northern Europe as work animals. They pulled carts in coal mines. They could also go to other places that were too small for regular-size horses.

By the late 1800s, some mini horses were brought to the United States. These horses were used to pull carts in the coal mines of West Virginia, Kentucky, and Ohio as recently as the 1950s. By the late 1970s, mini horses were hugely popular. Many appeared in horse shows. Others became lovable pets.

Years of breeding have created the wide variety of mini horses we have today.

Some of them were set free to roam in the wild. The harsh conditions of the land made the horses very sturdy. In the late 1800s, a rancher named Juan Falabella bred local horses to produce the breed we know today. Falabellas have the graceful look of an Arabian horse with a sturdy build and thicker coat.

These two miniature horses are Falabellas. It is a very popular breed.

mini horse

pony

Far Out!

Mini Horses and Ponies

What's the difference between a mini horse and a pony? For one thing, size. A pony is a small horse, but not as small as a mini horse. Ponies must stand less than 58 inches (147 cm) tall. They usually have wide, strong bodies. They also have thick necks, big bellies, and short legs for their size. There are many different kinds of ponies. Some are taller than others. (They can differ by a whole foot!)

A mini horse cannot be taller than 34 inches (86 cm). It is smaller than the smallest pony. It looks exactly like a full-size horse, only smaller. It should not have short legs, a thick neck, or a big belly.

3

Ready for a Mini Horse?

Where do you buy a mini horse? This isn't the kind of pet you can pick up at the local pet store. In fact, many states have laws against selling farm animals in stores.

Before you decide to get your very own mini horse, check with your town to see if you are allowed to own one. A mini horse is considered a farm animal. You may need to get a special permit to keep one as a pet.

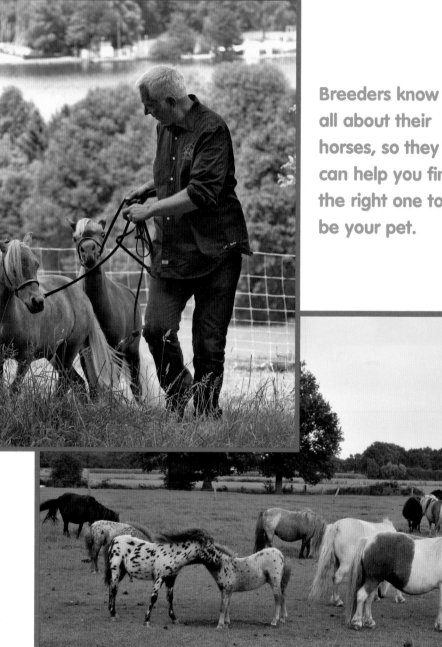

Breeders know all about their horses, so they can help you find the right one to be your pet.

Getting Your Own Mini Horse

A good place to get a mini horse is from a responsible breeder. You can find mini horse breeders on the Internet. Breeders generally take special care of their animals. They keep an eye on them and make sure they stay healthy. They also spend time with them to make sure they are gentle and tame. Breeders can give you information on the horse's background. In fact, you might even be able to meet the parents. Breeders can also answer any questions you might have.

A county fair is another place to find mini horses. People often try to sell their farm animals there. A horse auction is a good place to see lots of different horses, including minis. However, this is not the best place for a beginner. The auctioneer usually talks really fast and may bring up special

A veterinarian should look over the horse before you bring it home, just to make sure everything is all right.

horse terms that you have never heard before. It may be hard to understand what's going on.

No matter where you find your horse, it is a good idea to have the horse checked by your veterinarian. You should do this *before* you decide to buy the horse. You want to make sure the horse doesn't have any hidden health problems. Otherwise, it could cost your family hundreds or thousands of dollars in vet bills later.

Minis Are Like Potato Chips

Mini horse owners have a saying: *Minis are like potato chips; you can't stop with just one.* After all, they are so adorable. Who could resist? However, minis are not cheap. The price can range from hundreds to thousands of dollars. The really expensive ones are generally show horses, though. A mini without special training still makes a good pet. You can get one for several hundred dollars.

Mini horses are social animals. They *need* company. Spend as much time as you can with your horses. That will help them feel more comfortable with you. But no matter how much you try, you are no substitute for other horses. Mini horses are happiest when they are with other horses. If you cannot have another horse, make sure your mini has a friend, whether it is a miniature donkey, a llama, or even sheep.

If you do plan to get two mini horses, it is a good idea to get them at the same time.

Miniature horses like (and need) company.
This mini and goat are getting along well.

Dwarf Minis

Sometimes mini horses give birth to a dwarf. These horses are among the smallest of all. They often have physical problems, though. They may be born with very short legs or an oversize head and body, for example. They tend to have more health problems, as well, such as kidney disease. They might also have trouble breathing. Dwarfs generally don't live as long as regular minis.

Otherwise, your first horse may pick on the new one. When horses live in groups, there is usually a "boss." The others follow its lead. The one in charge may start kicking and biting others to show who's boss. The newcomer may get hurt.

Be careful if you do add a new animal to the group. Keep it in a separate stall or some other shelter and introduce it slowly. Have the minis spend a little time together each day until they get used to each other.

4

Caring for Mini Horses

The average newborn mini horse stands about
21 inches (53 cm) tall and weighs 18 pounds
(8 kg). It is so little you could easily scoop it up
and carry it around in your arms. You might even
be able to cuddle up with it while you watch TV on
the couch. Some people do bring their mini horses
inside the house from time to time. But mostly,
these pets should be kept outside.

Let's see what it takes to keep mini horses safe,
healthy, and happy.

They Grow Up So Fast!

Mini horses grow quickly. During their first year, they can grow 15 inches or more in height. At one year old, they are close to their full adult height.

Far Out!

Newborn miniature horses are tiny!

Although they need less room than full size horses, miniature horses still need space to run and play.

All the Comforts of Home

Mini horses need a lot less room than regular size horses. Like any horse, mini horses need a grass pasture. A backyard will do just fine. If it's big enough for a German Shepherd, there is plenty of room for a mini horse to run around and play. You could keep two or three minis on an acre of land.

Your mini's pasture (or yard) should have some shady spots for the horse to get out of the hot sun.

Far Out!

Can't We Get Along?

Can mini horses and dogs get along? Yes, they can, but they should never be alone together. Even a normally sweet-natured dog might suddenly attack the horse. Sometimes a dog's bark can frighten horses. The horse may panic and run away wildly. It could run into something and get hurt.

It is best to introduce the horse and dog slowly. Let them get used to each other. Always keep an eye on them and give both of them lots of praise when they get along.

Minis also need shelter to protect them from chilly winds or heavy rainfall.

Mini horses need to be kept in a fenced-in area. Otherwise, they could wander off and get lost or hurt. A fence is also good for keeping other animals out. The horses could get hurt or killed by wild animals, such as coyotes, or even stray dogs.

People use different kinds of fencing. A wood fence is a popular choice. However, you need to be careful that a mini cannot slip through the gaps. Unlike a large horse, a mini can get under the wood boards. The boards should be close together so the horse can't squeeze through.

A fence prevents your mini from getting lost and keeps it safe from other animals.

Wire mesh attached to wood posts is another choice. The spacing is small enough to keep a mini horse from getting a hoof tangled. A chain link fence would work as well. You should never use barbed wire. It could seriously hurt the horses.

For nighttime and bad weather, mini horses should have a shelter. It does not have to be a fancy stable. It can be a three-sided shed with a roof and an opening in the front. The shelter doesn't have to be very big. Inside, an 8-by-10-foot stall is a good size for a mini. Even a 6-by-8-foot stall is fine. Whatever shelter you choose, dry bedding, such as straw or wood shavings, can help keep the horses warm and comfortable.

An open front lets fresh air in, which is good for the horses. The horses can also come and go as they want. Sometimes they don't mind staying outside in the chilly air or rain. Their thick coats protect most minis from any kind of weather. They can usually stay outside without any problems.

Your mini needs a barn or shelter to protect it from rain and snow.

Eating Like a Horse

"You eat like a horse!" That's what people say when someone eats *a lot*. Large horses are known for eating a lot. In fact, that's one of the reasons it costs so much to keep horses. But mini horses don't really "eat like a horse" at all. They often eat as little as a tenth of the food that larger horses eat.

Still, mini horses will eat and eat and eat if given the chance. Overeating is a problem for many minis. If the horse starts getting a big belly, it's probably eating too much. Overweight horses can develop health problems. Horses need the right amount of food and exercise to stay healthy.

The pasture makes up much of their diet. Mini horses spend a lot of time nibbling on the grass. The grass should be mowed regularly. Horses prefer to munch on grass when it's short and fresh. (Fresh grass is softer and easier to cut with their teeth. Tall grass can be tough.)

Mini horses love to eat grass whenever they get hungry.

The short grass will also help keep the horses from overeating. Never feed a mini grass clippings. They can make a horse very sick.

Mini horses should also get a daily supply of hay and grains. They should be fed twice a day, once in the morning and then again at night. The average mini will need about one to one-and-a-half pounds (about half to three-quarters of a kilogram) of hay. They also need two to four cups of sweet feed, or grain.

Like any pet, minis love a tasty treat. Carrots, apples, and crunchy breakfast cereals all make good treats. But too many treats can lead to a weight problem. A little treat once in a while will make for a very happy (and healthy) horse.

There's an old saying, "You can lead a horse to water, but you can't make him drink." Horses are pretty picky about their water. Water is a very important part of their diet. But horses don't like muddy or dirty water. They should have fresh water at all times.

Horses also like their water at the right temperature. It has to be around 54 to 55 degrees Fahrenheit (12 to 13 degrees Celsius). In the winter, water can quickly get too cold or freeze, so the horses can't drink it. A horse's water needs to be changed often. A salt block should also be available at all times. Licking the salt makes the horse thirsty. Then it "remembers" to get a drink.

Basic Care

All horses have tough hooves. (A hoof is actually the hard outer covering of the horse's single toe. It's somewhat like our toenails.) Minis don't normally wear horseshoes like regular-size horses do. But their hooves still need special care. Mini horses must have their hooves trimmed at least every six to eight weeks. Many owners do it themselves. Some people give the job to the vet or to a specialist in hoof care. It's a good idea to handle a mini's feet when it is just a baby. Then it won't be frightened when its hooves are trimmed for the first time. Trimming is very important to make sure the hoof forms properly. Otherwise, the horse could have trouble walking.

The hooves should also be cleaned out regularly. Sometimes things get stuck in them, such as pebbles or other tiny objects. That could cause the horse pain.

Mini horses should have regular dental care, just as people do. A horse's teeth wear down over time from chewing. The uneven teeth may form sharp edges. This can be painful for the horse. The vet uses a special tool to file down the sharp edges. Other dental problems can develop as well. So horses should get their teeth checked every six months until they are two. Once a year is enough after that.

Far Out!

Horses with Toes?

Would you believe that horses used to have toes? That was more than 60 million years ago. The earliest horse, known as *Eohippus* ("dawn horse"), was actually very small, much like today's mini horses. It stood only 10 to 20 inches (25 to 50 cm) high at the shoulder. Its front feet had four toes. The back feet had three toes. Each toe had its own little hoof.

As the environment changed, so did the horse. Over a long period of time—millions of years, the horse's body changed. It became much taller—5 to 6 feet (1.5 to 1.8 meters) high. Its toes changed too. The original four toes on the front feet and three on the back feet joined into one toe on each foot. Each foot had a single large hoof.

Keeping your mini clean allows you to spend time with your pet. And it keeps it looking good.

Grooming is a very important part of caring for your horse. Brushing the horse's coat will help keep it clean and shiny. It is also a good way for your horse to get used to your touch.

Mini Babies

Some people choose to breed their mini horses. A female, called a mare, can have babies at around three years old. A male, called a stallion, is ready to breed around two years old.

Since mini horses are so small, the mares often have a difficult birth. Sometimes the baby horse—the foal—is too big for the mother to give birth to. Or the foal might get turned the wrong way. In these cases, the vet may have to do surgery to save the baby and the mother.

Unless you are an experienced breeder, it is probably best not to breed your horses. The vet can do surgery on your horses to make sure they cannot have babies. Stallions that have this surgery usually become calmer and gentler afterwards. A male horse that can no longer breed is called a gelding.

5

Training Mini Horses

Mini horses are known for being sweet, gentle animals. But they are not born that way. If horses are not trained properly, they can easily get out of hand. They may bite, kick, or charge at their owners. They may refuse to listen to commands and do whatever they feel like doing. This can make everyone's life difficult. And even worse, someone could get hurt. That includes the horse. This is why training is so important.

The first step in training is getting to know your horses. The more time you spend with them, the

Be sure to spend lots of time with your mini when you first get it. This will allow your pet to get used to you.

more comfortable they become with you. You should always be gentle. A horse is a lot easier to train when it learns to trust you.

The Basics

Training a horse is not always easy. Before you get started, read up on training mini horses. Find as much information on it as you can. Some people

Far Out!

Can You Ride Mini Horses?

Adults can't ride mini horses. A mini's back is not strong enough to handle the weight. Only young children should ride a mini horse. And the rider should weigh less than 40 pounds (18 kg).

Mini horses are often a big hit at birthday parties. Kids love to be around a horse that's just their size.

prefer to hire professionals to train their mini horses. But if you want to do it on your own, you could get their advice on training.

One of the first things you need to do is to train your horse to wear a halter. A halter is a thin strip of leather that you strap around the horse's head. Your horse needs to get used to wearing it. Once you attach a lead rope to it, you can lead the horse around to wherever you want it to go.

Using a halter allows you to keep your mini with you when you go out.

Tricky Minis

Dogs are not the only pets that can learn to do tricks. Horses are very smart, too. They have excellent memories for learning tasks. With the proper training, horses can be taught to do just about anything. For example, they can learn to come when you call them by name. You can take them on a walk like you would a dog. You can also

This trained mini is taking part in a miniature horse show.

teach them to sit, lie down, turn out the light, or pull up a blanket. For some real fun, you can teach your horse to play with a ball or even jump over obstacles!

Some mini horses have also been housebroken. They have been trained to paw at the door or make nickering noises when they want to go out. It is important to use lots of praise when the horse does well. Treats can be very helpful, too.

Helpful Horses

Don't be surprised if you see a blind person using a miniature horse instead of guide dog to get around.

Far Out!

Working Minis

Mini horses can learn to pull carts, wagons, or sleighs. They are very strong animals. They can pull a tremendous amount of weight—about 300 to 400 pounds (136 to 181 kg)—for several hours. A trained miniature driving horse can pull two adults for ten miles without any problem.

Some minis are trained to be seeing eye service miniature horses. They help their owners both at and away from home.

These horses can be specially trained to help blind people, as well as people with disabilities. Like guide dogs, miniature guide horses are service animals. That means that they are allowed to be taken in public places. They can even be taken on an airplane, on an escalator, or in a taxi.

Miniature horses can also make great therapy animals. Volunteer groups give the therapy horses special training to stay calm, gentle, and friendly with people of all ages. These minis help to cheer up sick people in hospitals and nursing homes. Patients look forward to visits from a therapy horse. Sometimes they even heal faster. Some patients who have not spoken for months or even years suddenly laugh and talk as they touch a visiting mini horse.

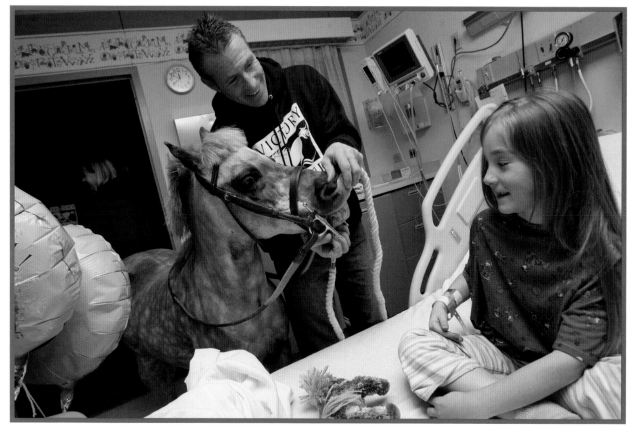

Specially-trained minis make visits to hospitals and nursing homes. They help make people smile.

Why miniature horses? For one thing, they are about the size of a dog. They are also very smart and can learn more than twenty commands. Minis are also a good choice for people who have problems with dogs. For example, some people have dog allergies. Some people have a strong fear of dogs.

One problem with minis is that they are not inside animals like dogs. Although minis can help people do things inside their house, the horses should be outside when they are "off duty."

* * *

Miniature horses are a great choice for horse lovers. Good things *do* come in small packages. Mini horses tend to be calmer than full-size horses. If you have always dreamed of owning a horse, this may be your dream come true. These sweet, gentle animals will be a part of your family for a long time—twenty-five to thirty-five years!

Words to Know

breed—To mate animals and raise their young; also animals with similar characteristics, produced by careful choice of the parents.

foal—A newborn horse.

gelding—A male horse that has had surgery to make it unable to breed.

halter—A thin piece of leather strapped around a horse's head and used for leading.

mare—A female breeding horse.

pasture—Land covered with grass.

stallion—A male breeding horse.

therapy animals—Animals such as dogs, cats, or horses used to help treat patients in hospitals and nursing homes and people with disabilities.

withers—The base of a horse's neck, where the mane ends.

Learn More

Books

Ellinger, Sabine. *Mini School: Train Your Mini to Be All He Can Be.* North Pomfret, Vt.: Trafalgar Square Books, 2010.

Hudak, Heather C. *Thumbelina: The World's Smallest Horse.* New York: Weigl Publishers, 2008.

Linde, Barbara M. *Miniature Horses.* Milwaukee, Wisc.: Gareth Stevens Publishing, 2011.

Van Cleaf, Kristin. *Miniature Horses.* Edina, Minn.: ABDO Publishing Co., 2006.

Smith, Donna Campbell. *The Book of Miniature Horses.* Guilford, Conn.: The Lyons Press, 2007.

Web Sites

American Miniature Horse Association
<http://www.amha.org/>

The Guide Horse Foundation
<http://www.guidehorse.org/>

The Miniature Horse.com
<http://www.theminiaturehorse.com/>

Index